Real Leadership in Real-Time

How to Lead With High Skill At High Speed

Dr. Tom Barrett

Real Leadership in Real-Time
Copyright* 2003 by Thomas J. Barrett, Ph.D.

Published by Business/Life Management, Inc.
ISBN 0-9641065-5-8
Cover design by Yellow Wire.

Printed in the United States of America.

How to Order More Copies or Get More Information
To order more copies of this book or be informed of its sequels; to receive Dr. Barrett's monthly leadership bulletins; or to contact him regarding speaking go to www.highspeedleadership.com.

For your convenience, order forms are also available in the back of this book.

What Others Are Saying...

...full of direct and simple truths that will help leaders re-baseline how to simultaneously take care of themselves and effectively lead others.

Al Serrano, Vice President Business Development DMS,
Northrop Grumman

Regardless of your position or title, *Real Leadership in Real-Time* will help you successfully address the leadership issues we all face on a daily basis.

Michael Firetti, Business Development, Cigital, Inc.

This book *is* Tom Barrett. That is to say, with qualitative examples and explorative questions, this book makes you listen to yourself and assists in exposing the leader inside.

JP Morgenthal, Author of Enterprise Application
Integration with XML and Java and,
Editor-in-Chief of "XML Journal"

A quick read with astute yet practical insights into the intricacies of effective leadership in real-time.

Ron Ralston, President and CEO,
Tightrope Communications

More comments...

The difference between winning and losing in business today is one word...LEADERSHIP. This book captures the essence of what it takes to become a great business leader.

Tom Mathews, Senior Executive Vice Chairman WFG, Inc.,
A member of the AEGON Group

...outlines clearly and powerfully the ingredients of excellent leadership. A must read book for all who are, or intend to become, exceptional leaders.

Palmer Suk, President Snelling Search of Vienna, Virginia

...a book that should be read repeatedly by leaders who want to focus on the critical aspects of skillful leadership.

Lori Stallard, Business Development Manager,
Telecommunications Solutions Team, GTSI Corp.

Dr. Barrett gives you a new way to look at yourself as a leader in any setting. He guides you to assess yourself, evaluate the situation you face, and prepare yourself for action—the right action. A sure-fire approach to effective leadership.

Mack Brewer, Principal Technical Advisor,
Northrop Grumman Information Technology, Inc.

To those who are, or aspire to be, extraordinarily
successful leaders

May the insights in this book help you lead with...
genuine confidence
unmistakable authority
real wisdom
and
unprecedented effectiveness

Tom Barrett, Ph.D.

Contents

Introduction

BEING A LEADER IS LIKE BEING a riverboat captain. If you don't know how to read the currents and get people to execute, you are dead in the water. Having raced kayaks, rafted through the Grand Canyon, and invested years working with political and corporate leaders, I know the similarities.

If you have ever spent a week camping and rafting through the Grand Canyon in the monsoon season, you know what I mean. It is extreme and it is awesome. Breaking camp at the river's edge at five in the morning, you feel bold anticipation and fearless excitement as you prepare for the day's journey down the river and into the rapids. But when the rapids appear in the distance, that fearless excitement gives way to rising anxiety. The rafters fall silent as the river begins to roar and the thunder and lightning above you crackle like rifle shots along the canyon walls. The same canyon that moments ago surrounded you with quiet and unparalleled beauty now engulfs you with a fierce and incomprehensible power. It cares not whether it sucks you down or spits you out at the other end.

In these frantic moments you shift from fear to total focus and massive execution. Through the visual chaos and raging water, you strain to hear the guide's rapid-fire instructions and follow them to the best of your abilities. When the river finally grants you safe passage back into calmer waters, all seven rafters lift their paddles to the sky in a "high seven" and cheer with the exhilaration of shared success. But the river does not allow you much time for sustained celebration. In short order, it will demand that you repeat the process.

Like a whitewater rafter, every successful leader knows what it is to cycle through:

**Anticipation * Excitement * Anxiety * Focus
* Execution * Exhilaration * Success**

The best leaders, the leaders who will thrive in the future, are those who...

- can read the ever-changing business currents
- know how to motivate others to anticipate success, sustain focus, and commit to massive execution
- recognize that leadership is far more than having core competency in a specific area
- are able to lead others in a workplace that is increasingly high-tech, high-speed, high-stakes, and high-stress
- understand the necessity of leading in real-time

The importance of accurately identifying business trends and helping others stay focused is nothing new—it's the speed at which we must accomplish these things to be competitive that's unprecedented. Bill Gates captures it well when he speaks of conducting business at the speed of thought. And this is not distant potential; it is emerging reality. Without question, the global business community is adopting a light-speed mentality—it sees the extraordinary value of technology that makes real-time communication possible across an entire supply chain. This technology, while extremely valuable, challenges leaders to think, decide, and act in real-time. Like a river guide navigating the rapids, leaders need to make critical decisions on the fly.

My goal in the pages ahead is to help you understand what it means to lead with high skill at high speed. If you are still trying to learn the essential elements of effective leadership, don't worry; whether you are new to leadership or a veteran, this book will do several things for you at minimum:

1. Strengthen your **knowledge base** of what it means to lead effectively in real-time.
2. Give you **executive insights** that enable you to "read the currents" and know what is happening with those you lead.
3. Provide you with **leadership skills** that are extremely important and immediately applicable.
4. Result in better **execution and focus** among those who work with you.

As the first in a four-volume series on leadership, this book will focus on two inescapable issues that many leaders overlook. The first is our own humanity as leaders. The second is what I call "the human equation." The dynamics of each are universal and constantly at play—I witness the same things working with a team of 50 people, a Fortune 500 company, or leaders in Congress. It doesn't matter if you work in the States, Switzerland, or Swaziland. These issues are present in your work environment regardless of your industry or business model. To maximize your effectiveness as a leader, you need to know them well and develop the wisdom to deal with them.

The subsequent books in the series will address these additional components of leadership:

1. How the best leaders stay focused and on task—and get others to do the same.
2. How leaders can learn to recognize their own talent and give themselves permission to lead with genuine authority and confidence.
3. How wise leaders turn their corporate culture into a "hidden revenue producer."

But first things first...

How to Get the Most Out of This Book

There are two things I know about leaders: they are usually very bright and very busy. Consequently, they are quick on the up-take and have no time to waste. I recognize that the more quickly readers can grasp an insight, the more swiftly it can be utilized. With this in mind, each chapter in this book is brief and written to stand alone. My goal has been to take profoundly important issues and put them in terms that are easy to understand. Feel free to grab the book and read just a few pages at a time. The quick investment will pay immediate dividends.

- Bring a quick mind and a light heart to this book. I intentionally wrote it with a lighthearted style. Relax and enjoy it. I don't know about you, but I find learning a lot more enjoyable when I remember to "lighten up." That said, don't be fooled by the reader-friendly style. This book is full of insights that are vital to skillful leadership. I urge you to take them seriously and apply them in your life.
- At the end of each chapter, you'll find a section called "Up Close and Personal." It consists of several thoughts and questions for you to consider. Please don't ignore these—it's this section that will help you custom fit each chapter's content to your individual situation.

- Keep the book handy so you can refer to it regularly. The insights here apply to the day-to-day, week-to-week leadership experience—they'll serve you best in the seemingly small moments that, over time, can make all the bottom-line difference. All leaders occasionally get lost in the fog of battle; it's easy to lose our perspective and make unwise decisions. Let this book serve as a global positioning system for you and those you lead.

The marketplace is like the Colorado River. It cares not whether it sucks you down or spits you out at the other end. But I care. Read the book. Apply its insights. Prepare to succeed as a leader. Some day, we will figure out the equivalent of the rafters "high seven" and we will celebrate your achievement together.

Tom Barrett Ph.D.
Vienna, Virginia

Chapter 1:

Da'Bears, Da'Bulls, and Da'Basics

DO YOU REMEMBER WHEN Mike Ditka coached the Chicago Bears and *Saturday Night Live* was an ingeniously funny show? During that time the show had a regular skit featuring several guys sitting around drinking beer and talking about sports. In every situation, no matter what the discussion, they always said the same thing. With perfect delivery, they'd respond to any question with one of two predictable answers: "Da'Bears" or "Da'Bulls."

Remembering Da'Basics of Leadership

Like professional athletes at the start of a new season, let's take a moment and remember "Da'Basics" of skillful leadership. Any of us can easily overlook them when we are moving at high speed and working with high stress—the "new norm" in many work settings. Increasingly, individuals and teams are being asked to be more productive, with fewer resources, in less time. This atmosphere makes it all the more important to remember that in business, just as in athletics, remembering the basics is a fundamental part of success. And they apply whether we are in da'bear or da'bull market.

Basic #1:

Remember the Fundamentals of Leadership

Following are some general descriptions of leadership I often use to kick-start dialogue with leaders:

- A leader is someone who knows where he or she is going and is able to motivate others to come along.
- Leadership is showing someone the way and then stepping out of the way.
- Leadership is providing vision, skill, and motivation.
- Leadership by influence is very different from leadership by title or position.

- A leader is able to answer three questions: Where are we going? How are we going to get there? Why are we doing it this way?

We can describe leadership in any number of ways and I don't mind what particular description you prefer; it's imperative, however, that you understand some basic qualities of leadership if you want to maximize your effectiveness as a leader. For starters, these qualities include awareness that leadership is about modeling, remembering what leaders are paid for, and remaining open to personal insights.

Basic #2:

Remember that Leadership is About Modeling

The next time someone asks what you do for a living, I suggest you answer by saying, "I'm a professional model." You may not walk down a runway modeling apparel—you may even think you have "a face made for radio"—but if you are in leadership, you do have a career in modeling. I assure you that when you walk down the hallways of your work place, you are modeling attitudes, beliefs, and convictions. You are modeling passion, vision, commitment, and work ethic. You are modeling pride in your company, products, and people. You are modeling what you value by the way you conduct yourself, manage your time, and execute your tasks and responsibilities.

As models, wise leaders remember three things:

1. Modeling is both the privilege and responsibility of leadership.
2. If you want your people to bleed then you need to hemorrhage.
3. Those you lead may be slow to duplicate the things you do well, but they will quickly identify and replicate those habits that may be less than beneficial to the business.

Basic #3:

Remember What Leaders are Paid For

Have you ever wondered what leaders are actually paid for? As leaders move into positions of greater responsibility, increasingly they are paid for their wisdom. *They are paid for knowing what to do while there is still time to do it.* If you are in a

position of leadership or if you aspire to one, remember that as a leader:

- You are paid for your ability to make wise judgment calls in the high speed of daily business.
- You are paid for your knowledge, skill, and insight.
- You are paid for your ability to direct, motivate,
  and lead others.
- You are paid for your creativity and critical thinking skills.
- You are paid for your problem-solving abilities.
- You are paid to keep yourself and others motivated, focused, and on task.
- You are paid to teach others to execute their
  responsibilities with passion, pride, and excellence.

Basic #4:

Remember that Secure Leaders Remain Open to Personal Insight

As leaders, it's important to have a clear understanding of what we do well and what we don't do
well. I see the same three types of self-assessment
distortion over and over again:

- Some people accurately assess their strengths but not their weaknesses.
- Some people accurately assess their weaknesses but not their strengths.
- Some people completely over-inflate their abilities and underestimate their weaknesses.

Each of these distortions hinders not just personal effectiveness, but also corporate productivity, profit, and culture. Still, as costly as these distortions are, they often persist for years because other people are reluctant to point them out. If you are in a position of senior management, let me ask you a question: When was the last time someone shot straight with you? The higher your position is within an organization, the less likely it is that anyone shoots straight with you. As leaders, it's easy to become accustomed to being the one dispensing insights and suggestions. The risk in that is losing the ability to be the recipient of information—especially when it may be needed more than it is wanted.

Remember that secure leaders are always open to new insights that can contribute to their personal effectiveness or to the success of their organization as a whole.

On a light note...

I appreciate the good-natured description of leadership used by Dr. Bill Turner. Bill is the James D. Hardy Professor and Chairman for the Department of Surgery at the University of Mississippi Medical Center. (Where the first human-to-human lung transplant was performed and the first heart transplant into a human.) This very gifted and tireless leader divides his time between managing a department that consists of forty-nine faculty members, forty-five residents, and two fellows while also performing surgery, teaching surgeons, chairing committees, hiring surgeons and support staff, etc. Bill describes leading this large group of surgeons as the equivalent of herding cats. If that is true, he is considered one of the best cat herders in the nation!

Can you relate to his description of leadership?

Up Close and Personal

1. What about leadership would you most like to learn in the pages ahead?

2. When was the last time anyone gave you honest insights to make you more effective as a leader? Has it been a week, a month, a year, longer? What did the person say? Was it accurate? Did you do anything about it?

3. Of the three typical self-assessment distortions, which matches your own tendency most closely? Do you see your strengths but not your weaknesses; your weaknesses but not your strengths; or do you over-inflate your abilities and underestimate your weaknesses?

4. Imagine someone asking you, "What are you paid for?" What would you say in response?

5. How is your "modeling career" going? What have you been modeling lately? How about today?

Chapter 2:

What Do You Fill a Room With?

LET ME ASK YOU A QUESTION: What do you fill a room with? If you have no idea what I'm talking about, you're not alone. Almost every CEO or senior executive I work with is initially puzzled too. They have no idea what I'm asking and wonder if it's some kind of joke. In fact, I am dead serious about this question, and the answer has everything to do with your personal leadership style and effectiveness. Knowing what you fill a room with is a significant component of wise leadership.

So let me ask you again: What do you fill a room with? Every time you enter a room, attend a meeting, give a speech, or chair a discussion, you are filling the room with some type of attitude, disposition, or demeanor. Whether you recognize it or not, other people unconsciously calibrate themselves according to the signals you send. Too many of us walk around like Typhoid Mary, the carrier of typhoid with no outward symptoms of the disease. She went around completely unaware of her impact on others as she transmitted a deadly airborne virus. As leaders, we need to know what type of "air-borne virus" we are spreading. We need to be aware of our environmental impact.

"As a leader, every time you enter a room, attend a meeting, give a speech, or chair a discussion, you are filling the room with some type of attitude, disposition, or demeanor."

Imagine that the EPA began compiling emissions data on leaders in an effort to understand what type of attitudes, behaviors, or characteristics they fill a room with—healthy and unhealthy. Their analysis of a leader's environmental impact would undoubtedly look for traces of the following:

confidence	belief	joy
hope	laughter	hype
tension	anger	boredom
passion	vision	skill
motivation	guilt	authority
dread	optimism	competence
leadership	vigor	commitment
tenacity	relentlessness	poise
inspiration	intimidation	calm
decisiveness	doubt	tentativeness
caution	"c.y.a."	wisdom
anticipation	expectation	sagacity
experience	authenticity	trust
stature	distrust	humor
dignity	team spirit	shame
service	cynicism	fear
stress	defensiveness	fragility
integrity	apathy	pride
competitiveness	laziness	disinterest
belligerence	frustration	fun

If the EPA did an environmental analysis of you, which qualities or "emissions" from the checklist would they detect? Are these emissions enhancing or hindering the work environment? Are others likely to receive them as helpful or noxious? How do you guess they're affecting your career? Is the impact positive or negative?

Two Examples of Environmental Impact

I love being around people who fill a room with an air-borne virus that transmits what Jack Welch calls passion and energy. There's no way to be around such people for long without "catching" some of what they have. Thankfully, there's no need to hope that your immune system is strong enough to resist their "virus"—if anything, most of us would welcome it!

- Phillip is one of these people. Phillip is increasingly recognized as one of the most gifted CEOs in the nation. He can "light up a room" when he speaks. It doesn't matter if he is speaking to employees, his board or senior management team, investment bankers, market analysts, customers, or other CEOs—like the old E.F. Hutton line, when Phillip speaks...people listen.

The important question, of course, is *why* people listen to him. Having worked with him for years, I know why. It has nothing to do with his speaking style or any kind of hype. It's because he fills a room with a genuine blend of intelligence, passion, and competence—and people perceive it readily. As a result, he has a profound environmental impact that is positively contagious. You can't help but "catch" some of what he has.

- Andy had a different impact on his environment. He was the chief legal counsel for a mid-sized corporation. His job was secure but his career was stalled. Andy sensed that his stature and value were not growing within the corporation, but he didn't know why. He asked me to analyze why his perceived value was not increasing. Since I was already on site at this company to analyze its corporate culture and leadership, it was easy to observe Andy. For several weeks, I watched him in senior management meetings, at company-wide meetings, and in the office corridors as he chatted with co-workers. I paid careful attention to the things he said and the way he said them.

Andy knew that I like to laugh and have fun even when doing serious work, so he wasn't surprised when I began my private analysis of his environmental impact by suggesting he change his name. He laughed and asked what I was talking about. I told him he should change his name to "Eeyore," the donkey with the gloomy disposition from *Winnie the Pooh*. I then went on to explain what he filled a room with. His voice, demeanor, and comments all filled the room with caution, doubt, and worry. I told him, "You sound like a professional whiner. Everyone is now calibrated to expect only negative statements from you. People stop listening at the very moment you start speaking. They don't want your dour comments or mood to rub off on them."

Like Typhoid Mary, Andy was completely unaware of how he was coming across to others. He had never paid attention to what he filled the room with. Once he became aware of the bad habits he'd slipped into and the impact they were having, he was free to get back on track as a valued player.

If you are serious about your development as a leader, focus on becoming aware of what you fill a room with. Over and over I've seen teams languish, sales lost, and deals die because of oversight in this critical area. I've also seen these trends reversed when people pay attention to it. So do your own environmental impact analysis—make sure you're filling the room with what you want to be.

On a light note...

Have you ever noticed that some people walk into a room emanating joy while others eliminate it? Some inspire laughter; others eradicate it. Some make you eager to stay; others make you eager to leave. When do you make your greatest impact—on your entrance or your exit? Let's hope it's the entrance!

Up Close and Personal

1. Look again at the checklist of "emissions" we can release into the environment. Take a moment and check the ones you think you exhibit.

2. From the qualities you checked, which ones do you like? Which ones might be minimizing your effectiveness as a leader?

3. Like Typhoid Mary, it's easy to be completely unaware of the impact we have on others. For the most accurate data, I suggest you videotape yourself in various meetings and work settings (if that isn't feasible, use a cassette recorder). Then study the video like a football coach preparing for game day. You may not like everything you observe, but remember that your goal is to continually enhance your effectiveness as a leader. Believe me, you can glean a wealth of information from this exercise.

4. What meetings do you have today, tomorrow, or this week that you need to take seriously? What do you want to fill the room with?

5. This week, make a conscious effort to observe what those around you fill a room with. What will you do with the insight you gain?

6. Mind if I meddle? Note what you fill your home with. Does your arrival trigger celebration, comfort, or caution?

Chapter 3:

Check Your Pulse

LEADERS CAN LEARN AN IMPORTANT lesson from diabetics—throughout the day diabetics monitor their blood-sugar levels. They pay consistent attention to what is happening within their bodies and respond accordingly. I encourage leaders to develop a similar skill: Learn to check your pulse on a daily basis. When I ask leaders if they know how to do this, I'm not wondering if they know how to determine their current heart rate. Rather, I am curious to know whether they've learned to pay attention to their own "state of being" and its impact on their behavior throughout the day.

Like shifting tides, there is a natural ebb and flow to our state of wellness. Our energy level and sense of well-being can fluctuate. Within certain limits, this fluctuation is the normal stuff of life; nonetheless, it can have a dramatic effect on our performance at work. Whether you realize it or not, you will bring the stuff of life into your workplace and it will color your view of people, problems, work, and the world. Leaders who learn to be aware of their "pulse" recognize this crucial distinction:

> **It is okay to have a bad day.**
>
> **It is not okay to manage a bad day**
>
> **badly.**

Don't Be the Last One on Your Block to Know!

Leaders often fool themselves into thinking that others don't notice when their personal life begins to leak into their professional world. They think they have a secure firewall that prevents others from having access to the "data" of their inner life. In truth, all kinds of people are seeing this data—and they don't have to hack their way into any database. How do they see it? It shows up in the leader's countenance, concentration, creativity, and coping style. It shows up in posture, facial expressions, gestures, and volume and tone of voice.

Ironically, a leader's family, executive assistants, and immediate colleagues usually know his or her pulse even *better* than the leader does. These people become skilled at recognizing the external indicators of the leader's internal pulse. They've learned to calibrate to it and make adjustments based on their observations. They decide if it is a day to be enjoyed while working hard or a day to work hard at being extra careful, staying on guard, and walking on eggshells.

I can't count how many times the executive assistants for people in senior management or members of Congress have told me, "Oh, we love when you spend time with the boss! He always comes back in a better mood when he has been with you." I don't know if it's because of the quality of my work or because I like to joke and have fun with clients, but it serves as a reminder that the colleagues of leaders often know the pulse of the leaders far better than the leaders themselves.

Taking your pulse involves being cognizant of three things:

- Your current disposition
- The cautions appropriate for that disposition
- The cause of your disposition

Know Your Current Disposition

Knowing your current disposition is the easiest of the three. This is as simple as taking a moment to note your mood or state of mind. Do you feel terrific or terrible? Are you up or down? Do you feel like Superman, able to leap tall buildings in a single bound, or does every problem feel like an insurmountable obstacle? Are you feeling strong and energetic or feeling tired and lethargic? Does your disposition suggest, "Bring on the day!" or does it have more of a Dirty Harry bent—"Go ahead...make my day!"?

One of the best times to take your pulse is while driving to work, especially if you have to contend with rush-hour traffic. You can use your response to traffic like a dashboard warning light indicating your current disposition. Are you relaxed and going with the flow or do you feel that every slow driver and red light is conspiring against you personally? Are you a little too quick to get frustrated, annoyed, or impatient, or are you singing a song and gladly anticipating the workday? Pay attention to these things, they reveal more about your current disposition than the traffic.

Know the Appropriate Cautions

Knowing your current disposition is one thing. Paying attention to how it might influence your day is quite another.

Some leaders are surprised to discover that they have to be most cautious when their disposition is at its best. Why is this so? Because some people are the least guarded when they are in their best frame of mind. In these moments they can give the store away. With too much zest and too little thought, they're inclined to give responses and make commitments that they later regret. See if you recognize any of the following:

- Have you ever been to a planning meeting in which participants, feeling strong and positive, made sales or revenue projections that were more SWAG than substance?
- Have you ever seen senior executives make promises of promotions, salary increases, or stock options in moments when they felt good, only

to retract them later, or, worse still, have little recollection of the promises they made?

- Have you ever seen a sales representative, in the excitement of closing a sale, give away a significant portion of the profit margin?
- Have you ever seen someone who, feeling too comfortable in a meeting, crossed the line by using humor that was over the edge?
- Have you ever over-committed yourself in the enthusiasm of the moment? Have you agreed to attend an event, give a speech, or chair a committee, only to find yourself thinking later with greater clarity, "I don't have time for this. What was I thinking? I must have been crazy to agree to do this!" You end up honoring a commitment that you never should have made in the first place.

Most of us have either witnessed these mistakes or made them ourselves. Over time, wise leaders learn to avoid such mistakes by using the caution appropriate to their disposition...even when it is excellent.

At the Other End of the Spectrum...

At the other end of the spectrum, leaders need to exercise appropriate caution when their disposition resembles Dirty Harry's. A negative disposition can skew judgment and make people speak with more haste and harshness than they should.

Have you ever seen a leader who was having a bad day rip the head off of someone over a minor issue? Ever see an anxious or angry leader become excessively critical, defensive, or hostile? Ever see someone having a tough day speak up at a meeting or send an instant message using razor sharp language? Ever see an employee having a bad day ruin a meeting, poison the work environment, or lose all customer-centered courtesy? When any of these things happen, it ain't pretty—and it isn't without a price. I have seen corporate morale, trust, passion, and culture decimated for months thanks to a careless leader failing to take a pulse check and acting without appropriate caution.

Know the Cause of Your Disposition

While knowing your current disposition and the cautions appropriate to it, it also helps to be aware of the cause of your disposition. Beyond just knowing *what* you are experiencing, do your best to understand *why* you are experiencing it.

There is an endless array of factors that can bend someone's disposition, mood, and mindset in one direction or another. Some of them are serious. Some are not. Common factors include:

- Being physically sick, tired, or run down
- An unresolved quarrel with a family member
- Concern for a child's health or behavior
- Stress over personal finances
- Pressure from an upcoming critical event
- Pressure to meet a deadline
- Unacknowledged depression, anger, or jealousy

When you can connect your current disposition to its root source, you have the advantage of greater awareness and control. It's the first step toward managing it effectively throughout the day.

The Perfect Storm

Leaders who have a particular combination of personal assets need to be especially careful to take their pulse. You fall in this category if you are all three of the following:

1. **Quick-minded**
2. **Authoritative**
3. **Articulate**

These are extremely valuable assets. Leaders who are quick-minded, authoritative, and articulate usually have little difficulty reaching swift conclusions. They form opinions quickly and express them effectively. Leaders with this collection of skills immediately know what they think and have few reservations about expressing their thoughts with conviction and clarity.

If you are gifted with this combination of talent, use it wisely. Under normal circumstances, these assets can be phenomenally helpful. However, under the wrong circumstances, these qualities can coalesce to form a perfect storm. How do these awesome qualities morph into lethal liabilities? With just a few drops of raw emotion such as anger stirred into the mix, this talent package can cause you to speak too soon, with too much force, and without considering the impact of your words. You can eviscerate people in a nanosecond. As a boss, you may be able to get away with it, but it is a long way from mature, wise leadership. If this becomes a pattern, those you lead will silently stop respecting and trusting you. They will merely tolerate you.

There are two reasons why I know the assets and liabilities of this leadership package. First, I have seen it in others many times throughout my career. Second, I have this package. I know first-hand the delight of using it well and the danger of using it poorly.

Whether or not you have this mix of skills, as a leader I encourage you once again—monitor your pulse and keep in mind that it's okay to have a bad day. But it is *not* okay to manage a bad day badly.

On a light note...

I recently had a humorous reminder of the impact of current disposition on how we approach our daily life and work. I was golfing with a CEO who is a dear friend of mine. We golf together regularly so I know that he loves to win and hates to lose as much as I do. On the fourth hole he pushed his drive and missed the fairway. It left him with a long second shot from deep rough and an uphill lie. After hitting this difficult shot, his ball landed on a downhill lie in a sand trap. I expected him to get aggravated but he remained unusually calm. Surprised, I commented on his being "Mr. Mellow" on the golf course. He laughed and sheepishly mentioned that he had just had some great sex with his wife before coming to the course. I kidded him about the pressure of a tough day...racing from intercourse to the golf course. At the end of the round, I was more than happy to take his money.

Up Close and Personal

1. What is your pulse today?

2. What has it been recently?

3. In what ways do you need to be careful when you are having a great day? Do you become too accommodating, too lax, or inclined to make commitments or use humor you later regret?

4. How do you need to be careful when you are having a bad day? Do you become more easily irritated, judgmental, or intolerant?

5. Do you have any idea what causes your most common dispositions?

Chapter 4:

The Secure Leader

DO YOU EVER WONDER WHAT some of your old friends from high school are doing now? Leo Romano is one of those "lost friends" for me. We went through a lot of our youthful indiscretions together.

I remember Leo becoming interested in karate while he was in high school. I watched him progress from a novice to becoming the Midwest black-belt karate champion. What intrigued me was the correlation between his fighting skills and his personal security. The more he developed as a karate expert, the more difficult it became to provoke him. Why did this happen? Because the more secure he became, the less he had to prove. And the less he had to prove, the more calm, unflappable, and deferential he became in his interactions with others.

This same principle is true for you in your development as a leader: The more personally secure you are, the less you have to prove to others. And the less you have to prove, the more you can forget about yourself and focus on the people or responsibilities needing your attention.

"The more personally secure you are, the more you can forget about yourself and focus on the people or responsibilities needing your attention."

Personal security is one of the overlooked variables that determine whether someone is highly effective or just high maintenance. Every day in corporate America, enormous amounts of time, productivity, creative thinking, and problem-solving ability are lost or wasted because of the psychological battles within and between people driven by insecurity. This is why senior managers often confide that the most difficult aspect of their job is babysitting the fragile egos and emotional needs of people around them—it takes too much of their time, focus, and energy. For an understanding of just how significant a difference personal security makes, compare the motivations of secure and insecure leaders:

THE SECURE LEADER...	THE INSECURE LEADER...
- gives praise to others	- seeks praise from others
- gives credit to others	- takes credit from others
- gives recognition to others	- needs recognition from others
- celebrates the success of others	- envies the success of others
- listens to others	- needs to be listened to
- works for the success of the team	- works for personal success
- is not easily upset or threatened	- is easily upset or threatened
- savors success privately	- flaunts success publicly

People in public positions of leadership who battle with excessive insecurity live with a painful private conflict. Professionally, they know they need to surround themselves with the finest talent available, but they find themselves personally threatened by exceptionally gifted colleagues. Consequently, they wind up in push-pull relationships with highly capable teammates because they simultaneously admire and fear them.

An Amazing "Coincidence"

When insecure people have the authority to hire and fire, it is amazing how many times they will discover supposedly legitimate reasons to find fault with highly capable individuals. I have seen numerous people harbor secret resentment over the success or talent of a colleague. And I've seen these people secretly rejoice over the "fall" of a colleague, even if the fall had to be "assisted." Unfortunately, this sort of relational tension and misuse of authority is not new. King Solomon clearly recognized it when he said, "The heart knows its own bitterness and no stranger shares its joy."

In building any team, organization, or business, we cannot afford to resent the talents of others. We need to be secure enough to recognize, respect, and embrace them. How do we do this? Be sure that our personal development is keeping pace with our professional development. The leaders who scare me the most are those who have seen the growth of their career far outpace the growth of their character. Leaders I respect the most are those who have matured proportionally in both areas.

Secure Leadership in Action

Marc Malnati is one of the people who models a secure sense of self and leadership without even knowing it. He's the owner of a very successful chain of restaurants in the Chicago metropolitan area known as "Lou Malnati's." Many people, including me, believe they serve some of the finest pizza in the country.

One afternoon, Marc and I were meeting for lunch in a hotel. Neither of us looked like a business owner. Both of us were wearing blue jeans, polo shirts, and leather jackets. As we were being taken to our table the hostess noticed that Marc's shirt had the logo for his restaurant imprinted on the front. She enthusiastically inquired, "Oh, do you work at Lou Malnati's? I love their pizza!" Marc smiled, nodded affirmatively, and only said, "I like their food too."

Why didn't Marc tell her that he was the owner of this entire chain of highly acclaimed restaurants? Why didn't he jump at the chance to tell her he was the "big dog"? Why did he pass up this unexpected opportunity for admiration or praise? The reason was simple: personal security. He had no need to grab the spotlight and put it on himself. He was as comfortable out of the spotlight as he was in it. Is it any wonder this man is genuinely respected and admired by all those who know and work for him?

Like Marc Malnati, the best leaders have a healthy mix of security and strength. I like to see leaders with: 1) An ego strong enough to lead, model, believe, and work aggressively, *and* 2) an ego that is secure enough to do these things with wisdom, humility, and the capacity to freely honor others.

Up Close and Personal

1. Can you handle someone else being in the spotlight instead of you?

2. Can you be glad for the talent and success of others or do these threaten you?

3. Is insecurity getting in the way of your ability to enjoy your past and current success?

4. Is insecurity creating an insatiable thirst within you that you hope will be quenched by more success, money, stock, or status?

5. When others contradict you or express opinions different from your own, do you see it as insubordination or disrespect or do you view it as healthy dialogue?

6. Have you noticed this paradox? Sometimes the best time to give people increased leadership is when they want it the least. These are the leaders who don't get enamored with their titles. They simply execute their tasks. They are aware that

leadership is more about responsibility than recognition.

7. A suggestion for the extremely talented: Learn to wield your talent with such elegance that it won't threaten those around you who lack the maturity and security to celebrate your skills and contributions.

8. By the way, don't confuse secure leadership with arrogant leadership. They're not even remotely related. Under the surface, arrogance is rooted in one of only two things: profound ignorance or profound insecurity. No exceptions.

Chapter 5:

Can You Get Out of the Spotlight?

AHHH.... TO BE AT CENTER COURT, on center stage, in the spotlight...it is a great feeling. I like it there myself. The more title or stature you have in an organization, the more likely it is that you'll be given the spotlight of praise, respect, and recognition—except when another "big dog" with a larger title is present!

Being comfortable in the spotlight is an important dimension of leadership. There can be a genuine benefit in believing that you belong in the spotlight and that you have something of value to contribute from that position. However, an overlooked but equally important component of leadership is the ability to get *out* of the spotlight.

As a leader, you engender loyalty, teamwork, and dedication when you are able to grab the spotlight of recognition and put it on others. This ability creates a culture in which individuals know that hard work, significant effort, and great results are honored, recognized, and rewarded. It creates energy, fuels motivation, and brings out the best in people. When leaders learn to focus the spotlight of recognition and affirmation on others it is often an unseen precursor to extraordinary team success.

Learn to Inspect Your Spotlight

If you are to grow as a leader, it helps to periodically inspect your spotlight. You might want to ask yourself, "How big is the beam of my spotlight?" To answer this question, picture an auditorium that is completely dark except for the beam of one spotlight shining down onto the stage. If this spotlight represented your ability to focus on others, how wide a beam would it have? Is it big enough that all the people who work for you or with you can fit into it? Is there room for praise and recognition of their ideas and labor, or is the beam only wide enough for you?

If you want to study one of the consummate examples of getting out of the spotlight and putting it on others, watch Joe Gibbs. Joe is the former head coach of the Washington Redskins football team and now owns a NASCAR team. Whether you see him in person, watch him interviewed on television, or read something he said, if you pay attention, you'll notice that all his remarks have one thing in common—he's always grabbing the spotlight of praise, turning it away from himself, and shining it on those with whom he works.

It's a relentless habit. You can't get Joe Gibbs to talk about himself. You can't get him to bask in the limelight or take credit for success. You can only get him to smile, laugh, and talk about his ability to hire people who are more talented than he claims to be. Reflexively, he redirects all accolades and admiration off of *himself* and onto his *team*. Is it any wonder that he's had world-class championship teams in two completely unrelated sports?

When I work with individual leaders or with senior corporate management teams, I want them to be comfortable in the spotlight; I want them to provide vision, skill, and motivation to their teams; I want them to fill a room with positive energy. I worry, though, when I see leaders move from comfort in the spotlight to becoming addicted to the spotlight. For some people, recognition and attention is like a drug—they can't get enough. Countless times I have seen people become so accustomed to being in the spotlight of praise and recognition wherever they go, they lose their ability to be comfortable outside it.

- Bob is one of the most visible people in corporate America. He is a CEO, single, good looking, lives in what can legitimately be called a mansion, and was one of the wealthiest people in the nation before the slide of his dot-com company. Bob recently went on a date with Stephanie. It must have been fascinating. For two hours he held the spotlight on himself while he spoke about his business, his success, his belongings, and himself. He was so accustomed to being in the spotlight that he assumed Stephanie was perfectly content with the privilege of being in his presence.

  By the end of dinner, Bob had not once asked Stephanie a question about herself. When she'd had enough, she stood up and stuck out her hand to shake his. With brilliant brevity, she simply stated, "By the way, my name is Stephanie." Then she walked away. Bob may think he is wealthy and smart, but I agree with Stephanie—I think he is poor and stupid.

- Greg is one of the most loyal, gifted, and dedicated people I have ever met in my years of working with people on Capitol Hill. He worked for one of the "Old Bulls," one of the venerable and once towering figures of the Senate. When the senator announced his retirement, Greg met with him and asked if he would consider endorsing Greg's run for a seat in the House. To the staffer's dismay, the senator felt threatened and became indignant. He accused the staffer of disloyalty and never fully trusted him again.

  What triggered such a selfish response? The senator had grown too accustomed to people investing their time and energy into making him look good. He couldn't tolerate anyone asking him to share his spotlight, even briefly. Gradually, he had lost the capacity to think of anyone but himself. He was stuck on center stage. Even when his career was winding down, he couldn't bear to have people in his employ thinking about their own lives rather than his.

Like the Wizard of Oz, the senator who seemed larger than life proved really to be rather small. He could have left a legacy in the life of a gifted, young politician. Instead, his legacy is buried in the annals of the Senate library and archives.

Watching what people do with the spotlight is fascinating. Some people are quite uncomfortable in it, others can't live without it, but the most balanced leaders learn to feel comfortable in the spotlight while always looking for opportunities to shine it on others.

Up Close and Personal

1. What do you think? Are you comfortable in the spotlight? Are you comfortable putting the spotlight on others?

2. Do you think it's your job as a leader to make others look good, or is it their job to make you look good?

3. Do you model a corporate culture in which people freely receive the spotlight of praise, or is it a culture that favors the spotlight of blame or shame?

4. What meetings do you have this week in which you can practice putting the spotlight of praise on others?

5. Is there a particular person, team, or division in your company that you need to honor and recognize? Think about it—who around you has been solving problems, bucking up, staying focused, setting the example of morale or productivity? Who has been taking up the slack, carrying the pressure, and just

flat getting it done? Why not honor them? Can you do it privately? Can you do it publicly? Can you do it in front of your boss?

Chapter 6:

Vision, Skill, or Motivation

BEING A LEADER IS MUCH LIKE being an escalator. You are a people-mover. One of your primary responsibilities is to move people to the next level of focus, execution, and success. You'll find the best guidance for doing this well in the old adage, "Listen more and talk less."

While many of us know this to be true in theory, it's easy to forget it while moving at full speed. For example, if you are in a position of senior management, there is nothing novel for you about attending a meeting. We have done it so many times, it's easy to walk into a meeting and "wing it." We just show up and jump in. While there is real value in being able to do this, we can become so *good* at winging it that it begins to diminish the overall quality of our leadership. We fall into the pattern of assuming too much and observing too little. We become so certain that we know what needs to be said that we stop paying attention to what needs to be *heard* by those we lead.

It's rare that individuals and teams will directly verbalize what they need. They are not going to openly tell you. In fact, they may not even know themselves. But if you will slow down and listen carefully, they will let you know what they want or need. You will sense it if you pay attention to their words, attitudes, and actions. Fortunately, it usually isn't very complicated. Like a restaurant menu with very limited choices, you will be astonished at how often those needs will be satisfied by one of only three selections: vision, skill, or motivation.

If you want to increase your effectiveness as a leader, learn to ask yourself a vital question while interacting with others. Silently ask yourself:

What does this person (or group) need from me right now? Is it vision, skill, or motivation?

When you begin to ask this question and become "spot on" with your answer, your insightfulness in managing those around you will grow exponentially. Consider the following three leaders—they each faced similar problems and were perceptive enough to see exactly where their teams needed support.

- Don is president of a telecommunications division. He was aware that his VP of sales was getting frustrated as he waited for large multi-million-dollar customers to "sign the deal" and cut a check. After spending significant time, effort, and money on these deals, the VP was beginning to doubt whether the protracted sales cycles would ever end. He was also beginning to doubt himself.

  How did Don handle this frustrated VP who was beginning to lose hope and doubt his abilities? He restored the *vision* of the VP. How did he do this? He reminded this key player of the big picture and assured him that he was doing the right things to move the deals along; that the contracts and revenue were imperative to the company's financial profile and market value; that closing these deals would be a cornerstone in his career and future value in the marketplace; and that he had no doubt that this VP *would* see the deals closed. The vitality of this VP returned with his vision.

- Tracy is senior VP of sales for a company in the Midwest. Her company is young and still waiting to get traction in the marketplace. As she watched her sales team, she noticed that they were getting tired from endlessly trying to introduce potential customers to their product with minimal results.

  How did Tracy handle a sales team that was increasingly frustrated? She focused on their *skills*. She implemented what she called a "See, Show, and Share" training. She cleared an already full schedule to make time to see how each interacted with potential customers. Then she showed them how to do things more effectively by letting them observe as she made calls herself. Finally, she helped each person on her team cultivate the individual skills they needed to improve their success rate. As the skills of the team improved, so did their attitudes and results.

- Paul, the CTO of a technology company, observed that one of his program managers was becoming increasingly frustrated and impatient with the engineers who reported to him. How did Paul handle the situation with his program manager? He restored his *motivation*. Paul knew that this program manager had been working incredible hours under enormous pressure as his team tried to produce the company's newest software. He could see that fatigue was beginning to directly impact this manager's perspective.

So what did he do? He told the manager to clear his schedule for the upcoming Friday. When Friday morning arrived, Paul met the manager and said, "Let's get out of here." He took the manager out for a round of golf and then told him to go home Friday afternoon and forget about work. He also told him he was not to report to the office until Tuesday morning. With a simple but brief respite from the intensity of his work, this program manager saw his motivation immediately return.

Whether or not you have the luxury of authorizing someone to take a day off, none of us as leaders can afford to overlook the importance of carefully monitoring those around us and supporting their vision, skill, or motivation as needed. For myself as a leader, I like to periodically remind myself of what each of these is and why each is valuable.

The Value of Vision

Late in her life, Helen Keller was asked if there was anything worse than not having eyesight. She responded, "Oh yes. It is to have sight without vision."

What is vision and what does it do? Vision allows people to envision the future. It is a sneak preview of potential realities for those who stay on task. It is seeing the big picture or the macroview of things to come. It is knowing with certainty what will occur tomorrow if we are diligent today.

The power of vision is its ability to give people hope and direction. It can infuse people with the will to work because they can see how today's efforts will bring them incrementally closer to what they want in the future. The more clearly people see the future, the more confidently they work in the present. To visionaries, the future is so real and so close to being within their grasp that it overrides whatever minor hassles they may be encountering in the moment. In short, clarity of vision is what keeps teams in a state of excellence instead of a problem state. It is what keeps them feeling strong and upbeat rather than down and discouraged, even when they are on a stretch of road where nothing seems to be falling into place.

The Value of Skill

What is skill? Skill is expertise, proficiency, and competence. It is knowledge of what to do and how to do it. It is the ability to successfully perform one's tasks or responsibilities. As leaders, we need to keep in mind that many people don't lose heart in their work because they lack vision, commitment, or motivation. They lose heart because they get tired of failure. They grow weary of "striking out."

Imagine what it would be like to be a major league baseball player. Initially, it would seem pretty exciting to most of us. But what if you were a major league player who struck out every time you were at bat? Eventually you would begin to dread game days instead of looking forward to them. In those times, you wouldn't need a pep talk, nor would you need pressure or guilt to remind you of your unacceptable batting statistics. What you would really need is a batting coach! The primary issue would be your swing flaws, not your drive or desire. If you could correct your swing, your attitude and motivation would immediately take care of themselves.

The Value of Motivation

Motivation. This is a great quality. It is drive, desire, and determination. It is the "fire in the belly" that makes people want to stay on task. It moves people to do something new or different. It is the fuel source that helps them sustain focus.

Motivation has two sources—one is internal, and the other is external. The most profound and lasting motivation comes from within ourselves. People who tap into their own private wellspring of personal motivation are unstoppable. They know what they want and why they want it.

Insightful leaders respect and find ways to tap into the individual motivations of those they lead. To accomplish this, they attempt to observe if this person or team is motivated by...

- Recognition
- Revenue
- Affiliation
- Challenging, meaningful work

- The prospect of a promotion
- Having their ideas or contributions respected and utilized

Learning to impart motivation to others by knowing what fires them up is much more elegant than attempting to motivate externally with the fear of being fired. Remember that leadership is providing vision, skill, and motivation with real-time awareness of which one the person or team you are leading needs most.

Up Close and Personal

1. You can't impart what you don't possess. What is the current level of your own personal vision, skill, and motivation?

2. Which of the three do you need the most right now? Why? Why is it lacking?

3. Think for a moment about the people you lead. What do they need from you the most? Is it vision, skill, or motivation?

4. Which of the three do you most easily exhibit? Which one is most difficult for you to impart to others?

5. As you interact with others this week, practice the habit of silently asking yourself, "What does this person need from me right now? Is it vision, skill, or motivation?"

Chapter 7:

Be an "ACE"

HAVE YOU EVER MET SOMEONE who seemed larger than life? Some people seem as if they have somehow crammed five lifetimes into the span of one. The more time you spend with them, the more they amaze you with their array of accomplishments and vast experience. If they are gifted with a keen sense of humor, a great memory, and the ability to tell a good story, it can be absolutely captivating just to listen to them reminisce.

Joe Foss is one of these people for me. Whenever I walk away from time spent with him, my heart is filled with laughter and my mind is filled with awe. You might be wondering who this Joe Foss is and what he's done that makes him so wonderfully unique. For starters, he's as humble as he is accomplished. In addition to being the former governor of South Dakota and a retired Brigadier General, he was the first commissioner of the American Football League. He is also a world-class hunter who used to have his own weekly television show, *The American Sportsman.*

You may recall seeing Joe's picture on the cover of *LIFE* magazine. He is a confirmed WWII ACE—his flight-suit is on permanent display at the Smithsonian Air and Space Museum—and a recipient of the Congressional Medal of Honor. It's possible that you saw Joe recently on the national news as he explained, with his inimitable humor, how an overzealous airport inspector refused to let him pass through security because his Congressional Medal of Honor might be used as a weapon! (In the end, Joe won this battle too.)

It's unlikely that you and I will have as wide-ranging experiences as Joe Foss, but as leaders, we should all aspire to one of his greatest personal achievements: becoming an ACE. I don't mean the type of flying ace that has a confirmed number of aerial combat victories. I mean the type of leader that consistently exhibits three qualities when interacting with others. Being an ACE means that you...

- **Speak with Authority.**
- **Speak with Conviction.**
- **Speak with Enthusiasm.**

Authority, Conviction, Enthusiasm

Why are these three characteristics so important? Because the higher your position, the more people look to you for their own sense of direction, confidence, and well-being. Whether you know it or not, they are taking cues from you on the state of affairs in your company. They are drafting off of what you demonstrate and verbalize. And these, in turn, have an immediate effect on their confidence, morale, motivation, belief, expectations, and execution.

Let's briefly look at each of the three qualities:

- **Authority**: Real authority comes from the power of your person far more than the power of your position. It is an internal mindset within you that others detect almost immediately. This mindset suggests that you are comfortable, confident, and competent to manage the issues at hand. It is a sincere attitude that assures people you are up to the task. This attitude makes it self-evident that you can answer those three most basic questions of leadership: Where are we going? How are we going to get there? Why are we doing it this way? Genuine authority motivates people to trust and follow your lead.

- **Conviction**: What is it? It is unflinching belief, an attitude, a state of mind, unshakable faith, an internal confidence. It's the certitude that gives leaders undaunted courage and tenacity when they "hit the wall" in the corporate marathon.

All leaders and businesses periodically face critical moments. Conviction in those moments is the belief that we will survive, we will make the right decisions, we will weather this storm, and we will find a way. Conviction telegraphs to others that we will win; we will reach the next level of growth, profits, or market share. We are tough and we will triumph.

Most importantly, a leader's conviction inspires action and belief in others. It carries with it a palpable message:

Our business will work, so let's keep working.
Our business will fly, so let's keep focusing.
We expect to win, so let's keep executing.

- **Enthusiasm**: In general, I am a huge advocate of enthusiasm. I love to be around people who have it and I pity those who go through life without it. However, in the business world, I am *not* a fan of enthusiasm if it isn't grounded in authority and conviction. By itself, enthusiasm reminds me of its distant cousins: hype, smoke, and mirrors. The less substantive and more enthusiastic someone is the more cynical I become. On the other hand, I have great appreciation for leaders whose enthusiasm is rooted in sound thinking, clear vision, and a repertoire of experience that has seen potential become reality. This sort of genuine, justified enthusiasm is a powerful emotional component of leadership. It creates positive energy, resourceful mindsets, and can fill a room with vigor, vision, and belief. It releases people to perform at their highest levels.

Flight School Basics

Pilots like Joe Foss will tell you that there are some basic skills taught in all flight schools. One of these skills is knowing what to do when an aircraft stalls. Student pilots are instructed how to put their aircraft into a stall, get it out of a stall, and most importantly, how to avoid an unwanted stall.

Knowing what to do with a "stall" is just as important for businesspeople and their careers as it is for pilots and their aircrafts. I repeatedly observe highly capable men and women miss leadership opportunities or lose leadership effectiveness because they've entered into a stall. Most of these individuals have no idea what caused it or what to do about it. They just know that in their current position they are not gaining altitude and they are losing speed. Then they become even more frustrated when they observe less capable individuals taking advantage of the very career and leadership opportunities to which *they* aspired.

Chris was one of these people. He is a software engineer who was regularly entrusted with managing hundred-million dollar projects that were extremely technical, time-sensitive, and vital to his company's bottom line. Despite the enormous complexity and pressure of each project, he always delivered—yet he was never invited into upper management. He was always viewed as a good team manager but never seen as a significant leader or a major player.

One day, in a moment of candor, Chris asked me, "Tom, when will people in this company begin to take me seriously?" I could hear his frustration in the question. I had no doubt that he was eminently qualified to be in upper management since I'd repeatedly witnessed his technical competence, management expertise, and leadership skills. I also knew that he exuded integrity and fairness and was fully trusted and respected by those he managed. This guy was a complete package.

I liked Chris and I liked his question. Initially, he didn't like my answer.

Following are the highlights of what I shared. I told Chris that the truth of the matter is:

1. You are better than you know. And you are better than you show.
2. You are viewed as an awfully nice guy. You are not viewed as an ACE.
3. People will not take you seriously until *you* begin to take yourself seriously.
4. People won't view you as a player until *you* begin to view yourself as a player.
5. People are not going to see the depth of your competence or confidence until *you* begin to

show it to them. And you will not begin to show it to them until *you* begin to admit to yourself how extraordinarily gifted you truly are.

Currently, Chris is in upper management at one of the largest defense contractors in the world. Why? Because he took three life-changing steps:

- *He began to privately embrace his giftedness.*
- *He began to publicly exhibit his giftedness.*
- *He gave himself permission to be an ACE.*

I enjoy seeing people like Chris flying with the speed and altitude they merit. This is when they're at their best, most effective, and most fulfilled. But I am well aware that many gifted people fly far below their talent level. This is a loss not just to the individuals themselves, but also to their place of employment and to the world at large.

I plan to devote an entire book to this subject, but in the meantime, begin to practice giving yourself permission to grow in your stature and effectiveness as a leader. Find your voice. Start speaking with genuine authority, conviction, and enthusiasm. You may not have a life as colorful as that of Joe Foss, but you can still be an ACE!

On a light note...

Remember that being an ACE has nothing to do with how loudly you speak. Some of the most effective leaders I know rarely raise their voice. Avoid the naïve mistake of thinking you can demonstrate more authority, conviction, and enthusiasm by simply speaking more loudly. Leadership is not measured in decibels. It is measured in the external impact of your internal knowledge, competence, and character.

Up Close and Personal

1. Is there someone you particularly admire as a leader? The next time you are with this person, watch how he or she speaks and models authority, conviction, and enthusiasm. Is one trait dominant? Does he or she exhibit the other two?

2. What about you? If I had the privilege of observing you in your work setting, what blend of authority, conviction, and enthusiasm would I see in you? Which would be most evident? Which would be least evident?

3. Some people in leadership fall in the rut of being a "one-trick pony." They have authority, they have conviction, or they have enthusiasm, but not all three. This can be a significant oversight. Different people, different audiences, and different cycles of business life require different blends of these three leadership qualities. It is important that leaders develop each of these qualities while also learning which one is most necessary in

their particular setting. Do you have an important meeting today? What quality will you exhibit? Is it the same quality that the listeners need to hear or see?

4. As you think about becoming an ACE, please keep this in mind: While I am interested in helping people in positions of leadership understand how to motivate, influence, and communicate with others, I have *no* interest in helping them learn to fake or mimic an image, aura, or persona that's not genuine. I am not interested in helping people appear to be something they are not. My aim is to help you lead with genuine authority, genuine competence, and genuine character. Be patient with yourself as you work to develop these qualities. Growth and maturity in these areas take time.

5. Incidentally...

- I honor those who have peaked in their career and leadership effectiveness.

- I quietly chuckle at those who have bluffed their way into positions far beyond their leadership skills.

- I feel badly for those who have stalled in their career or leadership growth because they never gave themselves permission to be an ACE and a player in the game of life.

- I get excited about those who are becoming an ACE and flying with confidence in their professional lives.

Where are you in the above list?

Chapter 8:

Face It, Fix It, or Exit

HAVE YOU EVER BEEN AROUND leadership teams that are highly skilled, intensely focused, and passionate about success? This is what makes the work environment crackle with positive energy and expectation. You can't help but enjoy a day in that kind of dynamic atmosphere.

But let's be honest—not every day is like this, even on the best teams. For many leaders, the worst days are those that involve speaking honestly to someone on their team about unacceptable performance or attitudes. This sort of news is neither fun to deliver nor to receive, yet every leader occasionally has to tell an employee to do one of three things: face it, fix it, or exit.

Like it or not, this is an inescapable component of effective leadership. One of the most valuable skills you can work to develop as a leader is that of delivering difficult messages in such a way that the listener can hear it, receive it, and respond— without being destroyed in the process.

Learning by Experience

In the beginning, many leaders try to avoid being truthful with others. Instead, they try to "flex," put on a game face, and act as though a teammate's poor execution or attitude is not a problem. In order to avoid conflict, they attempt to ignore behaviors, look the other way, and swallow their exasperation.

Eventually, leaders who do this learn the value of honesty the hard way. Out of frustration or exhaustion, they finally begin to speak candidly with the people who are not performing at acceptable levels. They do this as a last resort when they can no longer conceal their frustration. After cycling through this process numerous times, seasoned leaders begin to...

- Speak up sooner rather than later.
- Realize that problems they don't face won't be fixed.

- Recognize the difference between an incident and a pattern. They may choose to overlook an incident but deal directly with patterns that are problematic.
- Learn that being a leader is not always the same as being popular, well-liked, or a friend.
- Learn that if your goal is to be liked by everyone, it will be difficult to lead anyone.

These insights set leaders free to be increasingly straightforward with those they lead. They begin to be more candid, establish boundaries, and clarify expectations. They learn to address problems more swiftly and authoritatively, yet with increased skill and thoughtfulness. Over time, wise leaders ultimately comprehend that a vital aspect of mature leadership is knowing not just what to say, but how and when to say it. They learn to be truthful, tough, and tender all at the same time.

The Two Parts of Truthfulness: Content and Context

There are two parts to truthfulness that are often overlooked: content and context. The first deals with what we say, the second with the manner in which we say it. Many people get one part right but not the other; successful leaders learn to get both parts right.

The "Sergeant Joe Friday" Approach: Content Only

Some people are very good at delivering content. They have no problem saying hard-to-hear things to people. They just speak the unvarnished truth as they see it, with no regard for the impact of their words. Their style may be harsh, uncaring, and poorly timed, but as they see it, their task is simply to deliver the facts. This imbalance makes these leaders much less effective than they would be if they learned to share what they have to say in a softer style. Too often, instead of imparting wisdom, these leaders only inflict wounds.

Leaders who take this Sergeant Joe Friday "just the facts" approach could learn from the wisdom of King Solomon, who said: "A wise man chooses his speech judiciously and adds much persuasiveness to his lips." Clearly, as a leader, he understood the importance of choosing words with care, particularly when difficult things need to be said.

The "Good Ole Joe" Approach: Context Only

On the other hand, there are countless leaders who err on the other side of speaking the truth. They don't want to be Sergeant Joe Friday. They want to be the "good ole Joe." These leaders excel at the contextual side of leadership. They create a pleasant context for work, they like people and enjoy encouraging them, but they only want nice, positive interactions with others. They don't want to hurt anyone's feelings, and they want everyone to be happy. They avoid saying anything negative, even when it is important and true. As a result, many of the people they lead endlessly repeat the same mistakes because no one has told them what they need to hear, only what they *want* to hear. In the end, this is expensive for everyone.

Delivering Bad News: A Sample Format

When I have to give someone negative news, whether it's a member of Congress or a corporate leader, the format is always about the same. If at all possible, the conversation will be in person, in private, and it will go something like this:

"_____, do you know that I care about you?"
"Yes, Tom. I don't doubt that."

"Do you know that I am committed to you?"
"Yeah, Tom. I know that."

"Do you know that I want you to win as much as
you want to win?"
"I believe that, Tom."

"You know that I believe in you, at times,
more than you believe in yourself?"
"No doubt."

"I'm glad you know these things because
today I am going to hit you right
between the eyes. If you are serious about
wanting to be a winner, you need
to pay attention to…"

What am I doing in the above dialogue? I am balancing content and context, toughness and tenderness. I am speaking the truth in love. In effect, I am putting one of my arms around them as a friend while I punch them in the nose with the other. It is the depth of my caring that gives them the strength to handle the force of my message.

Before You Speak...

Please keep in mind that the right to say difficult things to people doesn't just come from a formal leadership title or position. Instead, the right to say hard things comes from having earned the right to say hard things. This right comes only after others know that:

- We care about them.
- We believe in them.
- We want to set them up to win.
- We are on their team and not just on their case.
- We are committed to their well-being.

When we have demonstrated these attitudes, people are much more inclined to respond well to what we have to say. At the same time, they'll be much more receptive to the kind things we say to them, knowing we will also share the difficult things.

My Hope for You as a Leader

Occasionally, all leaders need to tell someone, "It's time to face it, fix it, or exit." With respect to delivering this difficult message, I have two hopes for you as a leader. First, I hope that you will not avoid this responsibility. No leader, team, or organization can afford the luxury of lost time, marginal productivity, and poor attitudes. As you mature in leadership and become an ACE, I hope you will give yourself permission to speak with authority and conviction, not just enthusiasm. No one who aspires to effective leadership can rely singularly on enthusiasm as their only means of motivating others.

Second, I hope you'll keep in mind that while you have a responsibility to lead and a message to deliver, you also have a life in your hands. Be careful that you treat it with respect. Learn to be honest with people without shaming or humiliating them. Remember, mature leaders develop the ability to be truthful, tough, and tender. They know how to be candid without being cruel. They impart insight without inflicting unnecessary wounds. This is what makes them elegant and effective executives. It is also what makes those on

their team responsive, respectful, loyal, and productive. Pretty strong stuff.

Up Close and Personal

1. How easy is it for you to address problems and say difficult things to those you lead?

2. Do you avoid difficult conversations as long as you can, hoping they will "fix themselves"?

3. Do you err in the direction of being too tough or too tender?

4. Is your leadership style one of always trying to keep the peace and avoid conflict?

5. Is your leadership style one of confronting others when necessary but without thinking twice about the impact of your message on the recipient?

6. Can you address a person's behavior without attacking the person?

7. Is there an issue that you need to deal with in your work environment? Have you been dragging your feet in handling it? Why? Do you want to schedule a time to deal with it?

8. Mind if I meddle? How was conflict managed in the family you grew up in? This will have a significant influence on your current style of leadership and conflict management.

Chapter 9:

Thug
Leadership

WITHOUT QUESTION, HE WAS THE most dangerous person I saw all day—and my selection pool was fairly large. There were over 400,000 people on the mall in our nation's capital to celebrate the Fourth of July. This guy had an attitude that said loud and clear, "I'm big and I'm bad." At six-foot-six and well over 300 pounds, no one was eager to discover how much muscle lay buried beneath his gut. He sat astride his Harley-Davidson motorcycle wearing knee high leather boots, leather gloves, and chrome wrap-around sunglasses, silently daring any of us to make a wrong move.

I've been trained in psychological profiling, so I kept my eye on him throughout the day. I knew I was watching a thug; but I also knew that I was watching the most dangerous kind of thug. He was a thug with a badge, a Washington DC police officer. That badge had become both a cover and a justification for his private rage. In his mind, the badge authorized him to enforce the law at his discretion. As I observed him, he never seemed to tire of intimidating people while issuing tickets, fines, and threats. His goal was not to keep the crowd under control, it was to let everyone know that *he* was in control. From his perspective, we were on his turf and better not step out of line. None of his peers dared step forward to tell him that *he* was the one who was completely out of line. (Fortunately this motorcycle cop doesn't represent the great majority of his colleagues. Most police officers are honorable men and women doing a difficult job. I have enormous respect for their profession.)

Much like the motorcycle cop, I occasionally see people in the business world who exercise a similar form of control. They model what I call "thug leadership." If you have ever been around someone who uses thug leadership, then you already know: It isn't pretty. It isn't effective. It isn't impressive. It isn't professional. And it isn't without a significant price tag.

Elegant Wisdom versus Brute Force

Archimedes said, "Give me a place to stand and a lever long enough and I will move the world." He understood the elegant use of force to create massive movement. Wise leaders also understand how to use leverage—to create movement in the world of those they lead. They learn how to exercise what I call "elegant leadership."

Those who exercise thug leadership know nothing about the elegance of leverage or the genius of influence. They only know how to move people and things with brute force. They are like service repairmen who only know how to fix something by banging on it with a hammer; if that doesn't work, they get a bigger hammer.

In short, the difference between elegant leadership and thug leadership is like the difference between a surgeon using a scalpel to heal people and a madman running around with a samurai sword.

Elegant Leadership	Thug Leadership
Inspires others	Intimidates others
Earns respect from others	Demands respect from others
Respects others	Disrespects others
Affirms others	Abuses others
Builds people up	Tears people down
Is authoritative	Is authoritarian
Develops people	Destroys people
Leads by influence	Leads by force
Fills a room with positive energy and positive expectations	Fills a room with anger, fear, and tension
Knows how to be candid without being cruel	Doesn't know how to be candid without being cruel
Motivates others to pursue success	Motivates others to avoid failure
Solves problems without attacking people	Attacks people to solve problems

Why Do People Use Thug Leadership?

Laura asked her question out of earshot of her peers. I had just finished speaking to the senior management of the Global 1000 Company where she was employed. She wanted to know, "If thug leadership is so counterproductive, why do some people use it as a means of moving people to action?" It was clear to me that thug leadership was not her style of management but that she was observing it among some of her peers.

I told Laura that her question was profound and merited more time than I could give her. In the time I had, I shared just a few thoughts with her as to why people resort to thug leadership:

1. **They believe it shows bold, courageous leadership.** Some people naively believe that thug leadership is proof of their ability to be tough-minded and make hard decisions. They think thug leadership shows others that they're courageous, competent, and committed.

2. **Thug leadership is their default mode.** Some leaders who may not use thug leadership as their primary style of leadership still default to it un-

der severe pressure when they don't know what else to do. Instead of remaining calm, they become more harsh and demanding. When they fear missing important deadlines, they begin to lead with emotional impetuousness and abandon sound communication and leadership principles.

3. **They practice Machiavellian management.** Some companies make little pretense of valuing employees. They are run like sweatshops, elevating execution and profit above all else. To survive in this corporate atmosphere, some people in leadership "drink the cool-aide." Their behavior suggests a persona that's not really them. They abandon their own style, disposition, and values in order to "fit in" and be viewed as a team player—even if they have to become thugs in the process.

4. **They believe thug leadership works.** Some people honestly believe thug leadership is effective. They notice that when they "unload on people, read them the riot act, or tear 'em a new one," the recipients of this treatment become

quiet, attentive, and compliant. They notice that when they're extremely hard on subordinates in a meeting, it's usually followed by a flurry of activity. What thug leaders *don't* recognize is that the residual effect of their behavior is that employees are demeaned and demoralized. It erodes the respect employees have for themselves *and* the leader. Trust, loyalty, creativity, passion, employee retention, and long-term profitability all suffer.

5. **They are mercurial managers.** Some people resort to thug leadership for one simple reason: they are angry people on the inside. Like molten rock within the earth, their anger will gather pressure until it erupts through the surface and burns everything in its vicinity. Many people in positions of leadership are like metronomes to those who work with them. These colleagues know there is a predictable rhythm to the leader's eruptions. They learn to anticipate these eruptions and stay out of the line of fire during the explosions. They also learn not to trust the intervals between eruptions. They know it is just a temporary calm before the next storm.

(Incidentally, many national and corporate leaders are surprised to discover that private anger is what provides the fuel for their public or professional ambition. Mature people who make this discovery learn how to sustain their ambition while finding a healthier fuel source to motivate them. Others hold on to their anger and try to become more sophisticated at camouflaging it.)

6. **Because no one calls them on it.** Like the fable of the emperor's new clothes, some people in positions of authority use thug leadership because no one calls them on their ridiculous behavior. Like the motorcycle cop, no one dares to tell them they're out of line. Why don't people say anything? Because they sense that the leader lacks the ego strength to be corrected without becoming even more upset and hostile. They know that there would be "hell to pay" for being honest with a leader who is unsafe, unapproachable, and easily upset. So, like a dysfunctional family, they try to suck it up and ignore or tolerate the idiocy.

The Art of Cleaning Egg Off Your Face

Fortunately, in our moments of clarity, most of us know that thug leadership is a far cry from real leadership. We instinctively know it's neither elegant nor healthy. However, like junk food, there are times when it sure can look good. With the right mix of stress, fatigue, and frustration, it's tempting to resort to it as a shortcut to desired results.

So what should we do if we have slipped into the immature behavior of thug leadership? Be mature enough to admit it! Follow the witty advice of Frank Tyger: "Swallow your pride occasionally, it's not fattening." Some people in positions of leadership fear that acknowledging a personal mistake would lessen their credibility in the eyes of those they lead. They think it is a sign of weakness to acknowledge their own humanity. Consequently, when they do something inappropriate, they minimize the significance of their behavior and never own up to it. They simply keep moving forward and act like nothing happened. They develop forward-looking tunnel vision while being careful to rarely look back, up, or inside themselves.

If this is your style, keep in mind that most people don't expect us to be perfect as leaders; but they do expect us to be big enough to admit when we've made a mistake, blown it, or made a fool of ourselves (or worse still, a fool out of them). They want us to acknowledge when we have egg all over our face and ask their forgiveness for mishandling our leadership role.

When leaders mature to the point of being able to do this, they are often astonished to discover how gracious their colleagues can be and that their credibility is actually enhanced in the eyes of those they lead. Others who are too proud or insecure to admit mistakes are no longer viewed as insightful leaders. Over time, they are simply viewed as idiots!

On a light note...

Did you see the movie *What Women Want*? It's a romantic comedy starring Helen Hunt and Mel Gibson. In the beginning of the movie, the character played by Mel Gibson thinks he is the epitome of wit and wisdom. He has no doubt that people think he is a funny, loveable, awesome guy. As the story progresses, he develops the ability to literally hear what women are thinking. The more he hears, the clearer it becomes that their private views of him differ greatly from the way they act toward him publicly. To his dismay, he learns that he's not quite the superstar they pretend to think he is. Instead of thinking of him as an ACE, they actually think he is another three-letter word that sounds very similar to ACE. The same thing is true for thug leaders.

Up Close and Personal

1. Thug leadership isn't a one-person game—there's the thug, and there's the person bearing the brunt of the thug's "leadership." Which one are you?

2. Look at the list describing the differences between elegant leadership and thug leadership. Which one most closely resembles your leadership style?

3. Why do you favor the leadership style you use most frequently?

4. Do you know how to attack problems without attacking people?

5. Some political and corporate leaders are privately fueled with anger. Could you be one of these?

6. All leaders periodically end up with egg on their face. When you do, can you admit it? Is it more difficult for you to admit your mistakes to others or to yourself?

7. If you've been the common target of thug
   leadership in your work environment, why do
   you still work there? Do you hope things will
   improve? Are you afraid to risk change, afraid
   to lose your income or stock options? Do you
   need a reminder that no amount of income is
   worth your health, dignity, and self-respect?

Chapter 10:

More Powerful Than You Know

I DON'T KNOW ABOUT YOU, BUT it's easy for me to forget the simple truth that the little things we do are often the most important. This is particularly true when it comes to remembering that people need to feel valued and appreciated. At times I can be so intensely focused and busy that I overlook this simple fact. I recently received a much-needed wake-up call to this effect while on Capitol Hill.

Lessons from an Old Man

There is a common ritual on Capitol Hill: When a bell rings to signal a vote, all 435 members of Congress drop whatever they're doing and race like

Pavlov's dogs into the chamber to cast their votes. Only 15 minutes are allowed for a vote.

To expedite their arrival, a subway runs underground from the members'office buildings to the Capitol. This subway is a simple five-car train. It has two passenger cars in the front, one in the middle where the subway driver sits, and two more in the back. Six people can sit in each car for a ride that lasts only one minute.

Not long ago, I was in the midst of meeting with a committee chairman when a vote began. We hurried to the subway and jumped in. It was standing room only, packed with members of congress in power suits. They all looked very important—far too important to notice or speak to the driver of the subway, an old man about 80 years of age. As we made our one-minute trip, I began to talk to him over the noise of the train and the chatter of the members. I asked how his day was going, what time he came in, if we were having many votes, and if he knew what time we would adjourn for the evening.

When the train arrived in the Capitol, its doors opened and I was ready to jump off the train and hurry to the vote with the chairman. Just before I got out, I felt a tug on my suit sleeve. I turned and realized it was the subway driver. He didn't say a word. He just looked at me, smiled, reached into his pocket, pulled out two pieces of candy, and placed them in my hand.

Why did he do this? It was his way of saying "thank you." Thank you for noticing me. Thank you for treating me like a human being. Thank you for not acting as if I'm only a piece of the machinery. Thank you for not acting as if I am unworthy of being spoken to. Thank you for not treating me as if I am invisible. To this day, I still have those two pieces of candy. They serve as a reminder of what that dear old man taught me: the power of giving recognition to others.

Maybe You Need a Reminder Too

Sometimes as leaders we can't see the forest for the trees. Out of necessity, we get immersed in our management metrics and techniques. While focusing on the myriad tasks that demand our attention, we occasionally miss the obvious: the enormous power of simply recognizing others.

With this in mind, let me ask you a question: Are you aware of how powerful you are?

If you are in a position of leadership, you are like King Kong. What you say carries incredible weight. You can make someone feel absolutely fabulous with a brief genuine comment. There's a reason Mark Twain said he could run 30 days on the strength of one compliment. There is also a reason that the author of Proverbs wrote: "Death and life are in the power of the tongue and those who love it will eat its fruits."

What's happening around you today? Take a look—what great attitudes, abilities, or achievements do you see right in front of you? Since kind thoughts that go unexpressed have no positive impact, why not pass on your positive observation to the person or team you notice? Why not take a moment and send an encouraging e-mail, voicemail, or an instant message to someone? How about writing a brief note and leaving it on the person's desk? Why not discipline yourself to make this a habit? You can write a note in ten seconds and change the disposition of the recipient for ten days. That's a pretty impressive return on investment...

Keep in mind what wise leaders do:

- Wise leaders are always aware of "the human equation."

- Wise leaders remember the legitimate human need for recognition.

- Wise leaders look for ways to make people feel valued and appreciated for their talent, skill, and efforts.

- Wise leaders know that a microburst of affirmation from them can lift morale, improve focus, and create a state of resourcefulness in others.

- Wise leaders know that people who work in a resourceful state are more flexible, creative, and energized.

- Wise leaders know that those who work in a healthy corporate culture manage stress, pressure, and problems more effectively.

Additionally, wise leaders know that they set the tone for the attitudes and behaviors of the organization. They know they directly shape the work environment. In short, they understand that they are the pace car for corporate culture. They remember that being a leader means being a model and a servant. It means being secure enough to put the spotlight of praise and recognition on others. They remember that effective leaders provide three things: vision, skill, and motivation. And they understand why *affirming* others is a major part of creating motivation *within* others.

I know that your plate is full and that you already have plenty of things to think about. In spite of these realities, I encourage you to remember the power that comes with your leadership position. Remember the power of the tongue. Remember the power of a word of encouragement. Remember that you are like King Kong—and use your power wisely.

On a light note...

If you decide to make a habit of encouraging others, be sure you include those who work *for* you and not those for whom *you* work. When you do it for those who work for you it is an act of wisdom and kindness, but when you do it to those you work for, it's just "kissing-up." And let's be honest, whenever you kiss-up, it's not for the recipient, it's for you. Besides, your boss already gets too much of this. With half a brain, he or she can see through it immediately.

Up Close and Personal

1. Have you forgotten how powerful you are?

2. Have you been too busy to remember the power of an encouraging statement?

3. Who do you want to honor or recognize today? Why? What have they done that merits your comments? How are you going to tell them? (Face-to-face, a note, e-mail, voicemail, etc.) Why not do it right now?

4. As the pace car for corporate culture, what type of attitude have you been modeling for those you lead? What type of atmosphere do you facilitate?

5. Mind if I meddle? Have you forgotten the power of an encouraging word in your home? Have you forgotten that you are like King Kong? Why not take a moment today and tell your family what they mean to you? Remember, effective leaders don't live by intention...they execute.

Chapter 11:

Hit the Reset Button

IT WAS EARLY SPRING. The river was high, the water was rushing fast, and I was careless. While preparing for a kayak race, I shot over a dam and got sucked down into the undertow. Instantly, the water's force pushed me down and spun me in a series of uncontrollable backward summersaults. While trapped in the undertow, I couldn't tell up from down. Vertigo kicked in as the water churned around me and I lost all sense of direction. Just as the oxygen deprivation became life threatening, the water unexpectedly released its death grip and threw me to the surface 50 yards downstream.

As we navigate our way in the business world, it is easy to experience a form of "vertigo" and lose our balance and direction. The rapidly swirling mix of details and deadlines can fill our minds with such urgency that our sense of "true north" becomes increasingly skewed. We lose sight of where we are going or the manner with which we want to get there. When this occurs, it's helpful to hit the "reset button" and get a fresh perspective of what it means to provide skilled leadership.

There are multiple components to successful leadership that I'll address in detail in the sequels to this book. For now, let's return to the simple genius of effective leadership. Sometimes we make leadership far more complicated than it needs to be.

Lessons From One of the Greats

Some time ago, my wife and I were having dinner with another couple. In the course of our conversation, I discovered that the man had served on the personal staff of General Patton during his military career. Naturally, I was curious and asked many of the standard questions about this remarkable leader. I inquired about his personality, what it was like to work with him each day, and about his ivory-handled six-shooters. Then I asked if it was true that General Patton was as loved and respected by his men as history reports. Without a moment of hesitation he replied, "You bet!" Then I asked him to explain why that was the case. He thought quietly for a moment and then replied, "Because he loved his men and he believed in what he was doing."

Today's business climate is high-speed, high-stakes, high-stress, and increasingly high-tech. I know it's easy to get lost in the fog of battle. When you do, hit the "reset button" and go back to the basics: Care for the men and women you have the privilege of leading. And believe in what you are doing.

COMING ATTRACTIONS IN THE HIGH-SPEED LEADERSHIP SERIES

CONGRATULATIONS. You have just completed the first of a four volume series on leadership. The upcoming books will address three other vital aspects of effective leadership.

Volume two:

FOCUS!
(Where Fortunes are Won...or Lost)

SUCCESS OFTEN HINGES ON ONE elusive quality: the ability of organizations, teams, or individuals to remain on task and sustain relentless focus. Book two of this series will explain what focus is, why it is imperative, and why so few individuals and organizations ever master this insidiously simple concept.

More importantly, it will equip you with the skills needed by all leaders who want to learn how to get themselves, and those they lead, to remain resolutely focused on a daily basis and over long periods of time.

Volume three:

KNIGHT YOURSELF!
(How Leaders Learn to Believe in Themselves)

WHETHER IT IS IN THE POLITICAL world or the private sector, I have seen countless people with all the experience, competence, character, and skills necessary to be phenomenally effective leaders. But they lack one thing: a firm personal belief that they can "run with the big dogs" and "be a player" at much higher levels.

When individuals dismiss themselves as players in the game of life it results in talent that is unutilized and careers that are marginalized. However, when individuals begin to take themselves seriously, it becomes a catapult that thrusts their leadership effectiveness and career into entirely new heights. The third book in this series will explain how leaders learn to genuinely believe in themselves, lead with real authority, and maximize their ability to influence, motivate, and lead others.

Volume four:

CORPORATE CULTURE
(A Hidden Revenue Producer)

EVERY ORGANIZATION, WHETHER TEN OR ten thousand people, has a "corporate culture." While it has become politically correct to talk about corporate culture, few leaders understand why it should be a corporate priority. The reason is simple; a healthy corporate culture is a hidden revenue producer. It impacts productivity, profitability, atmosphere, morale, creativity, employee loyalty, and the disposition of every individual within an organization. Ultimately, healthy corporate culture transcends an organization and is externally detected by those who interface with any aspect of an organization's people, products, or services.

A dynamic and healthy corporate culture is not something that evolves unintentionally. This book will explain how it is shaped, developed, and modeled by leaders and assimilated at all levels of an organization.

Want an update?

Would you like to be notified when the above books become available? Send an email to: customerservice@highspeedleadership.com. Just write "notify" in the subject area. You will be updated on the release of each book and allowed to purchase it at a pre-release discount.

BARRETT'S LEADERSHIP BULLETIN

Would you like Dr. Barrett to help you and those on your team to keep growing and succeeding as leaders? Each month, via email, Dr. Barrett sends out *Barrett's Leadership Bulletin* to those who want to maximize their leadership skills.

To receive these free leadership insights, send an email to: bulletin@highspeedleadership.com

Request to be put on the bulletin list and you will begin to receive these monthly executive insights.

Share It With Others

Quantity	Item Ordered	Price Per Item	Total
	REAL LEADERSHIP IN REAL–TIME (hardback book)	$17.95	$
	REAL LEADERSHIP (audio book on CD) Available Fall 2003	$18.95	$
	REAL LEADERSHIP 10 Pack of Books	$15.95 each	$
	REAL LEADERSHIP 20 Pack of Books	$14.95 each	$
	For Large Quantity Discounts Contact: customerservice@highspeedleadership.com SHIPPING & HANDLING (one book) Select shipping method __UPS Ground ($5.50) __UPS 3 Day Select ($8.00) __UPS 2nd Day Air ($11.50) __UPS Next Day Air ($22.50)		$

ORDER TOTAL $_____

Check#_____enclosed for $_____(payable to Business/Life Management, Inc.)

Charge my: ❏ American Express   ❏ Discover
             ❏ Master Card   ❏ Visa

Account No._____Exp. Date_____

Print name as it appears on card_____

Signature_____

Address_____

_____

Phone_____Fax_____

Mail Orders to: Order Online:
Business/Life Management, Inc.   www.highspeedleadership.com
1501 Black–Eyed Susan Lane
Vienna, VA 22182   Fax Orders to: 703-759-4578

This offer subject to change without notice.